Living Dialogue

Chiara Lubich

Living Dialogue
Steps on the Way to Communion among Christians

Preface by
Walter Cardinal Kasper

Introduction by
Archbishop Rowan Williams

New City Press
Hyde Park, New York

Published in the United States by New City Press
202 Cardinal Rd., Hyde Park, NY 12538
www.newcitypress.com
©2009 New City Press (English translation)

Translated by Frank Johnson from the Italian original *Il dialogo è vita*,
©2007 Città Nuova, Rome, Italy.

Cover design by Leandro de Leon

Library of Congress Cataloging-in-Publication Data:

Lubich, Chiara, 1920-2008.
  [Dialogo è vita. English]
  Living dialogue : steps on the way to communion among Christians /
Chiara Lubich ; preface by Walter Cardinal Kasper ; introduction by
Archbishop Rowan Williams.
      p. cm.
  Includes bibliographical references.
  ISBN 978-1-56548-326-2 (pbk. : alk. paper) 1. Ecumenical movement.
2. Christian union. 3. Church—Unity. I. Title.

  BX8.3.L8313 2009
  262.001'1—dc22

                                    2009005927

Printed in the United States of America

Contents

Preface 7

Introduction 11

1. Toward a Spirituality of Unity 19

2. Renewing the Churches and Society 37

3. Prayer for Unity 45

4. Unity and Jesus Crucified and Forsaken
   Foundation of a Spirituality
   of Communion 48

5. Living the Word — Way to Unity 67

Preface

The ecumenical movement, which significantly marked the Church in the XX century and continues to mark the XXI century, has many and various roots. Among these, deserving of a special mention is, for example, the experience of the missionaries, who witness to the fact that the division among Christians is the greatest obstacle for mission in the world. But then there are the difficulties concerning mixed marriages between Christians; the sufferings of Orthodox, Protestant and Catholic Christians during the Second World War in the trenches and bunkers under aerial attacks; and the most dramatic experience of all, in the concentration camps, of a common resistance against a brutal neo-pagan regime. All this brought about an awareness that what unites Christians is much more than that which divides them. Anyway, in the last analysis, as the Second Vatican Council observed (see *Unitatis Redintegratio* 1: 4), the deep desire to bring about the unity of all Christians corresponds with an impulse coming from the Holy Spirit that urges us to go ahead on the ecumenical way.

This spiritual dimension of ecumenism had already been recognized by Paul Couturier (1881–1953), one of the most important pioneers of the Week of Prayer for Christian Unity. He it was who drew our attention to the fact that the words Jesus said on the eve of his passion and death, and left to us as his testament, are not a commandment, but a prayer directed to the Father. Thus, the deep soul, the very essence of ecumenism, is participation in this prayer of Jesus. And this is why we can be sure that everything we ask in his name will be granted to us, where and how God wishes (cf. Jn 14:13).

This prayer of Jesus, therefore, is the starting point from which the essential aspects of a spiritual ecumenism are derived. Such a prayer cannot be just a profession of the lips made up of many and carefully chosen words (see Mt 6:6). To associate ourselves with Jesus' prayer means rather to pray in the spirit of conversion; it signifies a purification of the memory and mutual forgiveness, in the attempt to overcome past misunderstandings and prejudices, in the effort to build trust and genuine friendship. There can be no ecumenism without personal sanctification and conversion.

In his prayer, Jesus does not ask for just any kind of unity, and certainly not for an enforced, mechanical or, worse still, a totalitarian union. Nor does he ask for a purely organizational or administrative union. Jesus wants the same unity that exists between him and the Father. This is why we must aspire to the original and exemplary model of the Trinity to bring about a unity-*communio* in love. Love does not depersonalize things by absorbing them, nor does it level them by making them all the same; rather it brings the greatest freedom and joy, by bringing to complete fulfillment those it embraces. Consequently, we are talking about unity in diversity.

Unity in love cannot be a mere institutional reality. John Paul II pointed out that an institutional *communio* without a spiritual *communio* would be a mechanism without a soul. Spiritual communion means welcoming others as brothers and sisters, sharing joys and sufferings with them, carrying each other's burdens (see Gal 6: 2), making their desires and their worries ours, making space for them and offering them friendship, considering their gifts as our treasures too, to bring to fruition together (see *Novo Millennio Ineunte*, 43).

If we look at recent developments and at the current situation where many people feel a spiritual vacuum left by modern secularization and are searching for a deeper fulfillment, we can see that spiritual ecumenism, as defined by Vatican II, is accepted more and more as being the soul of ecumenism (see *Unitatis Redintegratio*, 8). Today much more could be done than we normally do. And if we did all that it is possible to do today, it would be a great step ahead. So, spiritual ecumenism can help us to overcome weariness and discouragement and lead us, full of hope, on the way of the future. It can give fresh motivation and a new impulse to our search for unity.

This book by Chiara Lubich, founder and leader of the Focolare Movement which is committed to ecumenism all over the world, offers us profound and precious ideas, starting with that of the forsakenness of Jesus on the cross (see Mk 15: 34). The Pontifical Council for the Promotion of Christian Unity receives it as a welcome support to its own efforts in favor of the unity of all the disciples of Christ.

Walter Cardinal Kasper
President of the Pontifical Council
for the Promotion of Christian Unity

Introduction

The modern Christian prays again and again for unity among believers; the last hundred years have seen a previously unimaginable passion developing for the reconciliation of separated Christians, and every Christian leader in the world is bound to make reference to this and to endorse such a passion.

But it is all too easy to think of this as somehow not much more than the negotiating of a comfortable consensus. What Chiara Lubich's writings — and the whole witness of the Focolare Movement — challenge us to is the discovery of what unity really means: not simply unity between believers, but the unity that alone will heal the terrible and murderous conflicts between human beings the world over. From the very beginning of the Movement, the governing theme and calling has been the call to "make yourself one." And from the very beginning, Chiara has insisted that this first and foremost involves dispossession. Each of us stands in a condition of separateness, clinging to our markers of identity; and these markers of identity readily become defenses and barriers against each other.

To "make myself one" is not simply to strip away what makes me who I am; I couldn't do that even if I tried. And reconciling love comes from the real and distinct subsistence of a person made in God's image, not from a psychological vacuum. But it does involve stripping away those habits that allow me to anchor my security in what sets me apart from others. Only so do I become reliant on God alone, and become the agent of his love, not of my own good will, moral energy or spiritual resourcefulness. In this way only do I share in Christ's act — Christ making himself one with humanity, in a process that culminates in his dereliction on the cross and his cry of forsakenness.

So Chiara can write, in a memorable and definitive phrase, that "we need to know how to lose God within us for God in our brothers and sisters." As Christ himself empties himself of anything that could be called a private or self-enclosed relation to God the Father so that he may be at one with the dark and confusion of the human relation to God, so too for us (Phil 2). And as Christ rises from the dead not simply as a human individual resuscitated but as the Head of the Body, the community of the new creation, as the giver of the Holy Spirit, so we, in passing through this painful dispossession, enter into the new network of relationships that is the realm of the Spirit, in which there is no longer any intimacy with God that is not also intimacy with and compassion for the human other.

So it is that the life of God the Holy Trinity acts itself out in our lives. We are taken into Christ's desolation, with our defenses broken down, our habits of isolation and superiority challenged at their root. As St. John of the Cross said, over four hundred years ago, Christ is never more actively doing the Father's will than when he enters into the powerlessness and darkness of his death; so we in sharing his cross open ourselves to the Father's will, with our confidence in our own resources taken away. And when this happens, when God's love is allowed to move in us, it is the Spirit that begins to work, binding us not only to the Father through Christ but to one another in Christ. As we begin to receive Christ from each other in mutual love, we are led into a deeper level of joy than we could have imagined, something that goes far beyond mere feelings of well-being.

"Love must be distilled to the point of being only the Holy Spirit," writes Chiara; "It is distilled when it passes through Jesus forsaken." The simple but devastating truth is that God will fully act and live in our world when and only when we ask God to be himself in us — not for benefits and comforts and securities of any sort but for himself. And this is frightening to ask because it seems to be launching us into uncharted waters. As individuals we can only gain the courage to begin and to pursue this calling as we grow into the life of the Body and learn from those who have stepped out before us — above all from the saints and especially from Mary.

There will be some non-Roman Catholic readers who find themselves surprised, even shocked, by the central importance of Mary in Chiara's exposition. But she makes it absolutely clear why this is so: we have, she says, too often approached Mary as if she were not herself a disciple — the first "follower" of Jesus. The whole life of the Church of God is, historically speaking, rooted in her discipleship. She makes room in her heart and her body for Christ to be born. She experiences the threat and terror of being with Christ as the Holy Family flees into Egypt, leaving the slaughtered innocents behind. She faces the suffering of apparent separation from her son in his adult ministry, yet follows still, uncomprehending. She takes her stand with him in his desolation; and then, as Chiara wonderfully puts it, she becomes more than just a "follower." As she waits with the apostles for the gift of the Spirit, she enters the new creation where she with them is "transformed into him" by the gift of the Spirit. With all the company of Christ's people, she makes real the Body that is his beloved community, as she once made real the physical body of God's Son in her consent to the angel's message.

The human intimacy between Mary and her Son must have been an extraordinary thing, as Chiara reminds us. Yet when we travel with her into the mystery of Christ's desolation and resurrection, it is not simply a human intimacy that we are given. Like her, we receive a hidden life that will gradually transfigure every aspect of our being. So too, we should not be too fixated on having an imagined human intimacy with her. She goes on "mothering" the Church, and, like a mother, most of her work is out of our line of sight. She pours in her strength, her gentle love, her nourishment, whether or not we understand her or sense her presence like that of another person. She is our sister in faith as well as our mother; but much of the time we experience her in this latter role even as we recognize how we stand alongside her, because she has laid the foundations of faith for us in her journey. Scripture tells us little about her, little of the sort that would enable us to celebrate her great heroic holiness or her miracles. The great Catholic novelist, Georges Bernanos, commented that Mary in the Bible works no miracle except to be the place where the greatest of all miracles occurs, the Word of God becoming human. In this "poverty" of hers, she opens the door of grace to us and shows us an essential dimension of the love of the Trinity. It is like a mother's love in that it is rooted in the absolute bestowal of life, something deeper than any single limited gift.

The Focolarini are called to be a "living rosary"— that is, they are to be walking Mary's path. They are to be followers of Jesus; they are to be people in whom Jesus comes to life through the Spirit; they are to be a place where God's absolute gift of life can come through into the world, bringing others to new birth and feeding them with the glory and strength of God made flesh. Mary, says Chiara, lived "between two fires," the Spirit and Christ — the Spirit bringing Christ to life in her, Jesus himself calling to her as a human other to love. And so we live also between two fires, the inner attention to God's love in silence and adoration and the Jesus who dwells in our midst if we are met together in his name, that is, loving one another (Mt 18:20).

"Between two fires"; that is an unforgettable evocation of what it means to live and pray as a Christian. And the stark honesty of Chiara's description of the cost we must face in this condition prevents what she writes from being sentimentally consoling, or the emphasis on Mary being some kind of regres-

sive pietism. As Chiara says, this is very much a spirituality for our age, when we cannot avoid or lie about
the depth of human suffering, mental and physical,
that disfigures the world. And the only response that
will really meet this is the response of God in Christ
— stepping over the boundaries, making yourself
one. "Jesus forsaken is the God of our times." This
brings no magical solution, no instant healing; but it
radically changes the nature of the whole world we
live in....

What the Movement is advocating on the basis
of Chiara's theology is not some ambitious plan for
religious domination, the denial of independence to
the world or an ignoring of the real and sometimes
tragic complexity of its affairs. It is simply a matter of
learning a few basic skills in daily living and human
relating, and allowing them to make a difference to
whatever broader responsibilities we exercise. When
we do this, we are likely to discover that far more is
possible than we ever dreamed. And — crucially — if
we are truly acting on the basis of "making myself
one," the effect is not to divide the world into the doers of good and those poor souls who are "done good
to"; it is to break the barrier, to allow real validity to
the experience of the other and to help the emergence
of mutual dependence....

All that Chiara writes here is about a very special
group of people in the Church — by which I don't
mean Focolarini, special as they are, but laypeople.
She is writing about the specialness of the ordinary
baptized man, woman and child, and she reminds
us more than once of the lay status of the saints,

including Our Lady. We forget so easily that Jesus himself was not a "professional" holy man, a priest or even a rabbi: he was a son of Abraham, a man born into the covenant people in order to extend that covenant to the ends of the earth and create countless more children of Abraham from every tribe and tongue. The distinctive vocation in the Church of the priest or of someone living a vowed life as a monk or sister is there to serve the calling of the whole people, whose collective calling is the great new fact that Jesus brings into being. Once again, we are referred back to ordinary skills, ordinary and simple disciplines for living, not exceptional techniques. This is about the life of the person in relationship, in family and society, letting himself or herself be molded bit by bit into that vital exchange of life and love that is Christ's Body, learning to allow God in his love to tell them who they are — not society or family, certainly not fashion or profession or race, or even religion in terms of human institutions. We are who we are as disciples not because we identify ourselves as belonging to something called "Christianity," but because we have come to life in relationship with Jesus, the maker of the world who stepped over the threshold dividing creator from creation and became one with what he had made. How extraordinary and how tragic that we can make even that into another defense, another way of occupying and defending safe territory.

But God remains, and God is faithfully ready to take advantage of even the smallest motion of real trust and love, to take any opportunity of bringing his life to live in our lives. Once again, we should remember that this is not about heroism, about exceptional and memorable deeds to be publicly celebrated. Just as much as St. Thérèse's teaching, this is a "little way"; and just as much as the "little way," this is a call to the full radicalism of the cross of Jesus. Because it is about two great facts — the unchangeable love of God for each person he has made and the unchangeable purpose of God to build on earth an image of his perfect Trinitarian life by coming to live in our hearts — the message of Chiara Lubich is unaffected by passing fashions of thought, politics, culture, and so on. But for the very same reason, it is sharply and sometimes uncomfortably contemporary; it offers the hope of transformation in even the most apparently unfree and dark corners of our deeply shadowed world. It sets before us a lifetime's work, yet it is never more than can be drawn out of the shortest and simplest passage of Scripture. And in all these ways, it is true theology — which must always be nothing more than a reflection on and an induction into true discipleship: into the indwelling love of Father, Son and Holy Spirit.[1]

Rowan Williams
Archbishop of Canterbury

---

1. An extended version of this text was originally published in Chiara Lubich, *Essential Writings* (London: New City 2007).

1
Toward a Spirituality of Unity

Address to the Bossey Ecumenical Institute, 26 October 2002.

I have been asked to address the topic: *Toward a Spirituality of Unity.*

This title itself reveals an aspiration, it speaks of hope. And I know how deeply it expresses the work and reflections of the World Council of Churches.

As we know, Jesus founded his Church as one, and Christians the world over profess in the Nicene-Constantinopolitan creed: "We believe in one, holy, catholic and apostolic Church."[1]

There is only one Church of Christ, then, which we enter through baptism, which is "the sacramental bond of unity existing among all Christians."[2]

We know, however, that it is not enough to be united spiritually in our common baptism. "The ultimate goal of the ecumenical movement is to re-establish full visible unity among all the baptized."[3]

This hope highlights the fundamental role of ecclesiology.

---

1. See WCC Faith and Order paper 153, *Confessing the One Faith*, Geneva 1991.

2. Pontifical Council for Promoting Christian Unity, *Directory for the Application of Principles and Norms on Ecumenism*, n.92.

3. John Paul II, Encyclical Letter *Ut Unum Sint*, n.77.

Yes, this is how it is.

But what kind of ecclesiology do we mean?

Many years ago, Cardinal Willebrands, in an almost prophetic way, wrote that "a deeper ecclesiology of communion is perhaps the great opportunity for the ecumenism of tomorrow. The restoration of the unity of the Church," he continued, "should be sought according to the directives of this ecclesiology, which is at the same time very ancient ... and very modern."[4]

Today the ecclesiology of communion (*koinonia*) has been accepted, in the various theological dialogues among the Churches, as the way to understand both the Church and ecclesial unity: "The Church finds its model, its origins and its purpose in the mystery of the one God in three Persons."[5]

Furthermore, currently, the Faith and Order Commission of the World Council of Churches is reflecting on the nature of the Church as it has emerged in the theological dialogues.[6]

Consequently, there is a question that keeps recurring here and there: can these valid insights into ecclesiology be translated into life?

This is why people are seeking an ecumenical spirituality.[7]

---

4. J. Willebrands, "L'avenir de l'ecuménisme," in *Proche Orient Chrétien*, 1975 n.25, p.14–15.

5. The Catholic-Orthodox Dialogue, "The mystery of the Church and of the Eucharist in the Light of the Mystery of the Holy Trinity," in Gros, Meyer and Rusch, *Growth in Agreement II. Reports and Agreed Statements of Ecumenical Conversations on a World Level 1982–1998*, WCC 2000, p. 655.

6. See World Council of Churches, Faith and Order, *The Nature and Purpose of the Church*, Paper n.181, Geneva 1998.

7. See Consultation on "Spirituality for Our Times" of the World Council of Churches held in Iasi (Romania) 1994.

In Italy, a Waldensian pastor affirmed that "the lack of an ecumenical spirituality makes our task much more difficult and burdensome."[8]

So we need an ecumenical spirituality, a spirituality of communion, a topic which has been discussed extensively at the World Council of Churches, expressing the need to live an ecumenical spirituality so as to give new impetus to the ecumenical movement.

Today ecumenists ask themselves about spirituality as a "new way of ecumenism," but they ask: which spirituality?[9]

Is there a spirituality of that sort available today?

There are praiseworthy efforts aimed at reaching this goal. Perhaps they are known to us, perhaps not, because serious things, the things of God, usually grow in silence.

If they are the effect of the Spirit, however, then unity is not only a dream or a utopia: it is a real possibility.

One spirituality generated by the Spirit — it is considered to be so by those who have the grace of discernment for us — is the one I will tell you about today: the spirituality of unity, fruit of a charism for unity.

I speak of it with great gratitude to God, because it is his gift.

---

8. R. Bertalot, "La riconciliazione nei dialoghi fra le Chiese," in *Studi Ecumenici,* July — September 1996, p.359.

9. T. Vetrali, "La spiritualità nuova via dell'ecumenismo. Ma quale spiritualità?", in "Quale spiritualità per il terzo millennio?", *Quaderni di Studi Ecumenici,* 2000 Venezia, p.87–103.

It is a spirituality which is both "personal and communitarian," the spirituality of the Focolare Movement, one of the things brought about by the Spirit today in the Christian world; a spirituality whose effectiveness is already made evident by the fact that in different ways people from 350 Churches and ecclesial communities have made it their own.

A spirituality often regarded as ecumenical, and authoritatively defined as "robust"[10], therefore strong and demanding.

Here with you now I would like to look back over the years in which it began to take shape in the Christian world, and tell when and how its guiding principles became clear. I would like to specify the foundation stones upon which it is built and point out some of the effects it has had and continues to have.

But first, let's ask this question: a spirituality of communion, a spirituality of unity, on what should it be based? To whom should it give the first place in life?

Since it is a religious matter, logically the first foundation stone of this "spirituality of communion" can only be God, indeed God as he truly is: God as Love.

But how do we convince men and women today, including many Christians, to make God the Ideal in which they firmly believe when a thousand other things or persons around them attract and tie them down to the earth?

The Holy Spirit gave us the solution, taking advantage of an opportune moment and circumstances.

---

10. John Paul II to Catholic bishops, friends of the Focolare Movement, 16 February 1995, in H. Blaumeiser and H. Sievers (eds.), *Chiesa — Comunione*, Città Nuova 2002, p. 68.

In 1943 World War II was raging, scattering bombs, ruins, death everywhere and also in Trent (Italy) where certain young women were living, and whose story I would like to tell now.

The repeated air raids were gradually destroying the persons and things which formed the dreams, both big and small, of their hearts, such as having a family, furnishing a house, pursuing studies.... But ... that fiancé never returned from the front; that house was damaged; the war prevented attendance at the university.

Every circumstance affected these young women deeply. They understood that God was offering them a lesson: everything is "vanity of vanities" (Eccl 1:2; 12:8), everything passes away. This is what they said to one another.

Almost at the same time, however, in my own heart arose a question that touches everyone: "Is there a reason for living, a dream that does not die, an ideal to which we can give ourselves wholeheartedly, that no bomb can destroy?"

The answer was immediately clear: "Yes, there is. It is God."

There, in the midst of the destruction of the war caused by hatred, we were dazzled, as if for the first time, by the truth of who God is: "God is Love" (1 Jn 4:8). The light of the charism now gave us a very new understanding of God as Love.

We believed in his love with a deeply ardent faith. Consequently, if before we had thought of God as being distant and inaccessible, now we felt he was very close: he illuminated and transformed with his love all the circumstances of our life, whether happy, sad, or indifferent. Everything appeared to us as an expression of his love.

Our joy and amazement were so great that we did not hesitate an instant in choosing him, God-Love, as the Ideal of our life, just as we did not wait a moment to communicate to the people around us (relatives, friends) our great discovery: "God is Love, God loves us. God loves you, God loves you all."

To believe firmly in God who is Love, to choose him as the ideal of life, to believe that everything is love, all that happens to us, also because he makes everything work Toward good for those who love him (see Rm 8:28), is the first requirement, the first foundation stone of the spirituality of unity for whoever wants to make it their own.

We young women had, therefore, found the One to live for, God-Love. But what should our attitude be now, how could we put this new ideal into practice?

It became clear immediately: we had to love God in return. How could we do this?

We knew that Jesus had said: "Not everyone who says to me, "Lord, Lord," will enter the kingdom of heaven, but only the one who does the will of my Father in heaven" (Mt 7:21).

Doing the will of God was certainly the way to love God.

But who could reveal God's will to us? The will of God is expressed in many ways: by the Word of God, by one's state of life, by superiors, by circumstances, by one's conscience, etc.

We found the will of God expressed especially by the Word of God.

The sirens sounded as often as eleven times a day. We had to run to the air-raid shelters for cover without being able to take anything with us except a small copy of the Gospels.

We opened it and those words, which we had heard so often, were illuminated once again by the charism of the Holy Spirit, as if there were a light beneath them. They inflamed our hearts and impelled us to put them into practice.

They appeared to be unique (so different from those of all other books, even spiritual ones!); they were universal, made for everyone, and they were suited to all times, so for our times as well.

We started to live the Gospel, one sentence at a time.

One day we read: "Love your neighbor as yourself" (Mt 19:19). "Your neighbor" it said. "Who was our neighbor?" we asked.

We realized that our neighbors were right there next to us. Our neighbors were all those who had been struck by the war, who were wounded, hungry, thirsty, in need of clothes and shelter. We immediately devoted ourselves to them in many different ways.

The Gospel assured us: "Ask, and it will be given to you" (Mt 7:7; Lk 11:9).

We would ask on behalf of the poor and — something exceptional, considering the war — each time God showered us with all kinds of goods! One day in church, we asked for a pair of shoes size 8 ½ "for you" (in the poor man), and on the way out someone gave us those shoes.

We read: "Give and it will be given to you" (Lk 6:38). We gave, and each time we received something in return. Once there was only one apple in the house. We gave it to a poor man who asked for something to eat. On that same morning, a dozen apples arrived. After having given those too to the poor, a suitcase of apples arrived. This happened constantly.

These episodes, one after the other, amazed us and fascinated us. We realized, with surprise, that right now, Jesus was keeping his promises. Therefore, he was not only someone from the past, but of the present too. The Gospel was true.

This realization made us all the more eager to continue the new way of life we had recently set out on.

Our joy was great, contagious, and it increased when, again prompted by the Spirit, we communicated our experiences to one another. We also confided the things that were happening to us to those who were curious about our happiness in such sad times. In meeting us, others understood that Jesus was alive, and they followed him.

In a short time we were five hundred people of various ages and social backgrounds and among us all there circulated a vast communion of goods.

Living one sentence of the Gospel at a time, so suited to being translated into life, in order to re-evangelize constantly our way of thinking, willing and loving, and communicating our experiences to one another for our mutual edification, would be the third foundation stone of the spirituality of communion.

Of all the words of the Gospel — and we deeply loved all of them — (in fact, we thought that the Gospel was the only Rule of the new Movement), the charism gave special emphasis to those more specifically concerned with the love of neighbor: an ever-new love that is directed Toward everyone, that asks each one to take the initiative in loving, to love in a concrete way, to see Jesus in each neighbor.

Living out these characteristics of love taken from the Gospel is the fourth foundation stone of the ecumenical spirituality of unity.

Another circumstance from those early days of the Movement, painful in itself, was the harbinger of much light.

The shelter did not offer us much protection. Always in danger of dying, we asked ourselves: "Is there a word of the Gospel that is particularly pleasing to God? To make him happy, we would like to put that into practice before we die, at least in the last moments of our life."

The Gospel soon revealed it to us in the commandment that Jesus calls his own and new, and therefore special: "This is my commandment, that you love one another as I have loved you. No one has greater love than this, to lay down one's life for one's friends" (Jn 15:12–13).

Struck by the beauty, by the challenging commitment, and by the radicality of these words, we looked at one another and declared, under the action, we really believe, of an altogether special grace: "I am ready to give my life for you. And I for you. And I for you...." Every one of us for each of the others.

It was a solemn pact which would become the foundation of the entire Movement, whose members would later open up to universal brotherhood with men and women in the whole world.

From then on, while we were not asked to die physically, we lived this pact by always being ready (and always beginning again if we had slackened in this commitment) to die, in a sense, by annihilating ourselves spiritually in order to love our sisters and brothers, sharing everything with them, our few material and spiritual goods.

Mutual love among Christians, with the measure of giving one's life, is the fifth foundation stone, without which it is not possible to live the spirituality of unity.

But then, because of putting into practice this love for one another, the quality of our lives changed significantly. We felt a new confidence, a more determined will, a joy and a peace we had never experienced before, a fullness of life, an abundance of light.

Why? It immediately became clear to us when we read these other words of Jesus: "Where two or three are gathered in my name (in my love, say some Fathers of the Church), there am I in their midst" (Mt. 18:20).

Someone had very quietly joined our group — our invisible brother, Jesus. Thus the source of love and light was there present in our midst.

We intuited the infinite value of this presence and we never again wanted to lose it. Throughout all these years we have been committed to renewing this pact of mutual love so as to "generate" — as Paul VI said[11] — Jesus among us. This is the continual effort made by all those who live in the Movement.

Obviously, those who have not experienced this spiritual presence of Jesus in the midst of those who love one another, cannot fully understand what it is. Above all, they cannot appreciate what an "ecumenical resource" (if I may use this expression) it represents.

The fact is that the Holy Spirit is offering us, during this period of transition, for ecumenical dialogues at all levels, the possibility of being more one in Jesus. In fact, he can be present spiritually immediately, if we want him and if we love one another, between a Catholic and an Evangelical, for example, between a member of the Reformed Church and an Orthodox, between a Methodist and an Armenian, or among several members of one Church or another.

And it is precisely this presence of his that enables all of us, the faithful of many Churches present in the Movement, to say that we feel like one Christian family, one family that no one will be able to separate because Christ joins us all together. This presence of his among us has inaugurated a new dialogue, that "of the people, " and it has given rise to a new life on the way to that full and visible communion to which we wish to contribute.

---

11. See Paul VI, Discourse to the Parish of S. Maria Consolatrice (Rome, 1 March 1964), in *Insegnamenti di Paolo VI*, II/1964, Libreria Editrice Vaticana 1965, p. 1073–8.

Jesus in the midst is the sixth foundation stone of the spirituality of communion.

But let's go back to the beginnings of the Focolare Movement.

One day while taking shelter from the bombing, we met in a dark cellar. We opened the Gospel and read: "Father ... may they all be one" (Jn 17:21). It was Jesus' prayer shortly before he died. These were difficult and powerful words, but here again, we felt we could understand them, at least a little.

Not only that, but those words instilled in our hearts the conviction that we were born for that very page of the Gospel, almost as if it were the Magna Carta of the Movement. We felt that we had been created to contribute toward the unity of people with God and with one another, and thus to fulfill God's plan for humanity.

Unity, as Jesus intends it, appeared to us as difficult to achieve, so we prayed, united, asking him to reveal the key to unity and, if it were his will, to make us instruments of unity.

Unity is the seventh foundation stone of the "spirituality of unity." It is typical, characteristic just like the other key point: Jesus crucified and forsaken, which I will come to in a moment.

Afterwards, our group was touched in a special way by another sentence of the Gospel: "Whoever listens to you [that is, the apostles] listens to me" (Lk 10:16). For us it meant listening to our bishop. We wanted to put this into practice at once; we introduced ourselves to the Archbishop of Trent, Carlo De Ferrari.

He listened, smiled, and then he said: "I see the hand of God here," and his approval, support and blessing accompanied us until his death.

This first approval on the part of the ecclesiastical authorities had a twofold effect: it assured us that the light we had followed was genuinely Christian, and it accelerated our pace. Then the approval of the Catholic Church arrived through the various Popes.

Profound and sincere unity with whoever in the Church represents Christ is the eighth foundation stone.

Happiness, discoveries, graces, the spreading of the word of God. This is certainly the Gospel life. But right from the start we understood that everything also had another side to it, that the tree has its roots. The Gospel covers you with love, but it also demands everything of you. The Lord permits trials which can, at times, take your breath away. But only by accepting and overcoming them is life fruitful.

"Unless a grain of wheat falls into the earth and dies, it remains just a single grain; but if it dies, it bears much fruit" (Jn 12:24). This is personified by Jesus crucified, whose fruit was the redemption of humanity.

Jesus crucified!

In another episode from those early months — a new circumstance foreseen by heaven — we had a new understanding of him.

We had learned that the greatest suffering of Jesus was when on the cross he experienced abandonment by the Father: "My God, my God, why have you forsaken me?" (Mt 27:46).

Deeply touched by these words, and being young and enthusiastic, but especially because of a grace from God, we felt a strong urge to follow him in that very moment of his abandonment. We saw in him the way marked out for us by God and we consecrated our lives to him forsaken.

Quite soon we understood that Jesus forsaken was the Holy Spirit's answer to our prayer: the way to bring about our Ideal of unity and love.

In fact, Jesus forsaken, who had experienced being distant from the Father because he had identified himself with the separation of human beings from God and from one another, overcame this immense trial by re-abandoning himself to the Father ("Into your hands I commend my spirit" [Lk 23:46]), showed that he was the remedy for every disunity, the key to unity with God and with one another.

But how can we, how can Christians make use of this key now?

An explanation is necessary here.

The Word of God, having assumed human nature in Jesus, also took upon himself each of our sufferings, he burdened himself with our sins, to the point of becoming "sin," although not sinner; he took upon himself all the divisions of the world (see Gal 3:13; 2 Cor 5:21).

It was for this reason that the heavenly Father permitted him to experience the abandonment.

But because Jesus covered himself with all our evils, we can discover Jesus himself, one of his faces, behind every suffering, behind any separation we experience. We can embrace him, in a sense, in these sufferings, in these divisions, and say our "yes" to him as he did. Jesus, in fact, facing such suspension, did not rebel. He accepted his extremely painful condition, entrusting himself again to the will of the Father.

If we do as he did, if we say our "yes," we will be reunited to him and he will live in us; we might still be suffering, but we will experience the risen Lord within us and peace will return.

Genuine, fulfilled Christians have acted as Jesus did. For instance, when Thérèse of Lisieux, a Carmelite nun of the Catholic Church, coughed up blood because of the tuberculosis that had afflicted her, she did not say: "I've coughed up some blood," but "my spouse, Jesus, has arrived." The blood was there, of course (and this was the human viewpoint), but it was also true that Jesus, having made that suffering his own, was presenting himself to Thérèse (and this was the viewpoint of faith).

In our experience, an ecumenical spirituality will be fruitful in the measure that those who dedicate themselves to it see in Jesus crucified and forsaken, who re-abandoned himself to the Father, the key to recomposing unity with God and with one another. The traumas, the separations that come between Christians will be dissolved in the warmth of their love for Jesus forsaken. This is a powerful contribution to the ongoing work of Church leaders to re-compose the visible unity of the Church, a gift which God himself will give.

This is why, I'll confide to you, as I did to the Second Ecumenical Assembly in Graz, that after forty years of ecumenical commitment, the Focolare Movement sees Jesus forsaken as the "star" for the ecumenical journey.

Indeed, the hearts of many already burn with enthusiasm for an effective ecumenism. Deeply touched by him, they do not flee from him, but love him and find in him the light and strength not to remain in the traumas and in the rifts caused by division, but always to go beyond them.

Jesus forsaken is the ninth foundation stone. The two most important aspects of the spirituality of communion are Jesus forsaken and unity.

And another foundation stone is a great love for the Holy Spirit, Love made Person.

Jesus gave the Holy Spirit to us when he died on the cross, and he filled the new-born Church with him at Pentecost.

The Holy Spirit binds the Persons of the Most Holy Trinity in unity, and the Holy Spirit is the bond among the members of the mystical Body of Christ.

Before concluding this overview of the points of the Movement's spirituality, I would like to say something about who Mary is for us. Because she is recognized by Christians as the Mother of God, proclaimed as such by the Council of Ephesus (431), and because she is the first Christian, we look to her as a model, the model of Christians. She is completely clothed with the Word of God. We can imitate her by living what she said: "Do whatever he tells you" (Jn 2:5) and by spiritually giving life to Jesus in our midst.

This is the "spirituality of unity" then, whose main points are: the choice of God-Love as the ideal of our life; doing his will; living the words of the Gospel; particularly emphasizing love; living out the new commandment of Jesus; "giving birth" to Jesus in our midst; achieving unity among ourselves; remaining in unity with our Church leaders; reliving in ourselves Jesus crucified and forsaken; loving the Holy Spirit. And imitating Mary.

However, since it is not possible to know this spirituality properly without knowing its effects, here are just a few of the many, already present in those early days.

In his prayer for unity, the Magna Carta of the Movement, Jesus had said: "May they too be one ... in us, so that the world may believe ..." (Jn 17:21). And this is what happened, even during the war, around us: people felt strengthened in their faith and began to believe again in God, or to believe for the first time; more and more people changed their way of life; many converted to God; commitments taken for him were reinforced; people returned to their own Church.

A few months later, people of all ages and from the most varied social backgrounds shared this Ideal and formed there, in the midst of the world, a community similar to that of the early Christians.

Then, in the course of the following years, this spirituality spread throughout the world like an "explosion" (as someone described it), first in Italy, then in Europe and finally in the other continents. Now the Focolare Movement is present in a hundred and eighty-two nations.

This spirituality has enabled the Movement to open, with very positive results, the four dialogues which are so relevant today: that in the heart of our own Churches; among various Churches and ecclesial communities; with the faithful of other religions; with men and women of good will who do not have any religious affiliation.

Furthermore, living the Gospel in this way is renewing and "inundating" the most diverse fields of human activity, not only those of theology and philosophy, but also the arts, economy, politics, medicine, education, etc.

Thus, it is something vast, a notable example of a deeper unity among Christians and of universal fraternity among many, realized in one part of the human race.

2

Renewing the
Churches and Society

Address given at Geneva, in the cathedral of St. Pierre, 27 October 2002, just a few days before the celebration of the anniversary of the Reformation, an occasion that involves all the Lutheran and Reformed Churches. In her initial greetings, before her talk, Chiara addressed them as "beloved brothers and sisters," wishing them "the best spiritual gifts" and declaring her wish "that Jesus be in our midst."

Next 3 November the anniversary of the Reformation will be celebrated here in Geneva, a religious celebration which I hope will bestow the best spiritual gifts on all the Christians of the Reformed Churches, my beloved brothers and sisters.

On that day, one word will resound powerfully: "reform."

Reform, a word that expresses the desire for renewal, change, almost rebirth.

A word that is special, attractive, that means life, more life.

A word that might also prompt a question: does the noun "reform," the adjective "reformed" apply only to the Church whose center is located in Geneva?

Or are these words applicable in some way to all the Churches? Indeed, were they not always characteristics of the Church?

The decree on ecumenism of the Second Vatican Council says: "Christ summons the Church, as she goes her pilgrim way, to that continual reformation of which she always has need, insofar as she is a human institution here on earth."[1]

And if we look carefully at the history of the Church, and in particular at the years in which we Christians were still united, we will see that Jesus, with the Holy Spirit, always intended, willed and oriented his Bride Toward a continual reform, encouraging constant renewal.

This is why, from time to time, the Lord sent on earth gifts, charisms of the Holy Spirit which gave rise to new spiritual currents or religious families. Through them he offered once again the sight of men and women who live the Gospel in a total and radical way.

This is how it is in our times too, dear brothers and sisters. There are dozens and dozens of charisms spread throughout the Churches which are capable of bringing renewal. By way of example, I will tell you about the one called the "charism of unity" which gave life to the Focolare Movement.

This ecclesial reality, in fact, although born in one Church, the Roman Catholic Church, is now made up of people who belong to more than three hundred and fifty different Churches and ecclesial communities.

Its abundant fruits, its expansion around the world in one hundred and eighty-two nations, and its being made up of seven million people speaking

---

1. *Unitatis Redintegratio*, 6.

ninety-one different languages, tell us that so far, thanks be to God, things have gone well for it.

Its aim is precisely that of working toward unity among all Christians and Toward universal fraternity among all men and women on earth.

Furthermore, this Movement is remarkably timely, as we will see by analyzing together something of the present-day situation of our planet.

We are all familiar with the United Nations World Summit on Sustainable Development which was recently held in Johannesburg and which was described as "an ecological conversion."[2]

It set before the eyes of the world the terrible statistics on poverty in which a large portion of humanity finds itself. Clearly, it is no longer possible to remain inactive.

We must learn, and the world must learn, to bear in mind the plan that God has for humanity and to live accordingly: we are all sisters and brothers, we are one family.

Furthermore, today as never before there is a danger of enormous gravity: widespread terrorism.

Thus, not only the thirty-four wars, the fruit of hatred fed by the widest variety of reasons, still today afflicting and tainting dozens of nations with bloodshed, but something much more serious, if eminent people also see this event as an implication of "the forces of Evil" with a capital "E." It is not sufficient to respond with human strength alone to re-establish

---

2. See Holy See Intervention at the World Summit on Sustainable Development on 2 September 2002, in *L'Osservatore Romano* English Edition, n. 37, 11 September 2002.

equilibrium and justice. We have to mobilize the Good, with a capital "G."

We need, as a starting point, to begin a new era supported by a shared prayer for peace and unity.

But this is not enough. We know the deeper reason for so much evil. It is the resentment, the compressed hatred and rancor, the desire for revenge which people have been harboring for years on end because of the division of our planet into two parts: the rich part and the part that is racked by poverty, at times, abject poverty.

So, we must treat one another as brothers and sisters; we need communion, solidarity, sharing. Goods must be shared out, but we know that they do not move on their own. We need to move hearts. Therefore, we need to see a great fraternity rise up in the world and — given that the problem is universal — a universal fraternity.

This is not a completely new vision. Witnesses in recent history like Mahatma Gandhi, Martin Luther King, Mother Teresa of Calcutta, the Dalai Lama and John Paul II have thought of it and deeply longed for it.

But more than anyone else, Jesus wants universal fraternity, given that he prayed: "Father, may they all be one" (see Jn 17:21).

In speaking of unity, he speaks of fraternity; as Christians, we can and must find the model of fraternity in the Trinity itself, whose life we can share, through our common baptism.

Unity — unity and fraternity.

Unity and fraternity which, because of the charism of unity, the Focolare Movement is particularly committed to achieving.

It witnesses and teaches that to live unity, one must start out from the love announced in the Gospel, that radical love which is so typically Christian. That love which, if it is welcomed with attention and diligence, and put into practice, can offer great hope for this moment in history. Indeed, it can become a further expression, together with prayer, of that Good with a capital "G" we have called upon.

It is not a limited love, like human love, which is often directed only Toward relatives and friends. It is directed to everyone: to the pleasant and the unpleasant, to the attractive and the unattractive, to fellow citizens and foreigners, to someone who belongs to my religion and to someone of another, to someone of my culture or another culture, friend and enemy.

Therefore, it is a love that imitates that of the heavenly Father who sends the sun and the rain on the just and on the unjust.

It is a love that urges us to be the first to love, always to take the initiative, without waiting — as human love would — to be loved. It is a love like that of Jesus who, when we were still sinners, and therefore not loving, loved us by giving his life for us.

It is a love that makes us consider the other person as ourselves, that makes us see in the other person our very own selves.

It is a love that is not made up only of words or sentiments; it is a concrete love, like that shown by Jesus when he washed the feet of his disciples and worked many miracles.

And although this love is directed to a man or to a woman, it leads you to loving Jesus himself in the person loved. That Jesus who considers done to himself whatever good or evil is done to our neighbors. He said this in speaking of the universal judgment: "You did it to me" (see Mt 25:40) or "You did not do it to me" (see Mt 25:45).

Finally, it is a love that, if lived by more than one person, becomes mutual, that mutual love which is the pearl of the Gospel and whose measure is to give our life: "This is my commandment, that you love one another as I have loved you. No one has greater love than this, to lay down one's life for one's friends" (Jn 15:12–13).

Those who have practiced this in the Focolare Movement, for instance, have experienced that love is the greatest power on earth: it unleashes the peaceful Christian revolution around those who live it, so that Christians today can repeat what the early Christians said centuries ago: "We were born only yesterday and we have already spread all over the world."[3]

This Christian revolution touches not only the spiritual realm, but it also renews all expressions of human endeavor: cultural, philosophical, political, economic, educational, scientific, etc.

Love! What a great need there is for love in the world! And in us, Christians!

All together we Christians of various Churches number more than a billion people. Such a multitude

---

3. Tertullian, *The Apology,* 37:7.

should be quite visible. But we are so divided that many do not see us, nor do they see Jesus through us.

He said that the world would recognize us as his own and, through us, would recognize him, by our mutual love, by unity: "By this everyone will know that you are my disciples, if you have love for one another" (Jn 13:35).

Consequently our uniform, our distinctive characteristic, was supposed to have been mutual love, unity. But we have not maintained full visible communion, nor do we have it now. Therefore, it is our conviction that also the Churches themselves must love one another with this love. And we strive to work in this direction.

How often the Churches would seem to have forgotten the Testament of Jesus, scandalizing the world with their divisions, while they should have been winning it for him!

If we look over our 2,000 year history, and in particular at the history of the second millennium, we cannot help but see that it has often been a series of misunderstandings, of quarrels, of conflicts which in many places have torn the seamless tunic of Christ, which is his Church.

Certainly, this was caused by circumstances: historical, cultural, political, geographical, social…. But it was also caused by the fact that among us there was a lack of this unifying characteristic typical of us: love.

And so today, as we seek to make up for so much evil, to draw new strength for a fresh start, we must put all our confidence in this evangelical love. If we spread love and mutual love among the Churches,

this love will lead the Churches, each one different from the other, to become a gift for the others,
as John Paul II hopes for in his book *Crossing the
Threshold of Hope*: "It is necessary," he writes, "for
humanity to achieve unity through plurality, to learn
to come together in the one Church, even while presenting a plurality of ways of thinking and acting, of
cultures and civilizations."[4]

Our world today asks each one of us for love; it
asks for unity, communion, solidarity.

And it also calls upon the Churches to recompose
the unity that has been torn for centuries.

This is the reform of all reforms which heaven is
asking of us. It is the first and necessary step toward
universal fraternity with all men and women of the
world. The world will believe, if we are united. Jesus
said so: "May they all be one ... that the world may
believe" (Jn 17:21).

God wants this! Believe me! And he repeats it
and cries it out through the present-day circumstances he permits.

May he give us the grace, if not to see all this
accomplished, at least to prepare for its coming.

---

4. John Paul II, *Crossing the Threshold of Hope*, Random House, UK, 1994, p.153.

3

Prayer for Unity

A prayer offered on 28 September 2002, at the World Council
of Churches in Geneva.

Jesus, here we are, those in charge of the World
Council of Churches, bishops of various Churches
who adhere to the Focolare Movement, and leaders
of the Focolare Movement itself. We have come together to get to know one another better, which we
hope is in accordance with your will.

We are here first of all to ask you for something
great, Lord!

You said: "Where two or three are gathered together in my name (in my love), there am I in the
midst of them" (Mt 18:20). Kindle in us all a great
fraternal respect, help us to listen profoundly to one
another, arouse among us that mutual love which al-
lows, indeed, which ensures your spiritual presence
in our midst.

Because we know, Lord, that "without you we
can do nothing" (see Jn 15:5).

But, with you in our midst, we will be given
light by your light and be guided on this day when
we will deal with an issue that touches us all and
that concerns especially you and your Church.

You know the various tasks we have in it, or better, the one yet varied and weighty calling laid on
each of us: to work, together with many others in the

Christian world, so that full and visible communion among the Churches may one day become a reality.

Even though this — we know — requires almost a miracle. This is why we need you, Jesus.

For our part — in this moment — before beginning such a demanding meeting, ever aware that we are "useless and unfaithful servants," we cannot help but open our hearts and reveal to you our deepest sentiments.

First of all, we feel the need to ask you for forgiveness on our own behalf, but also on behalf of our Christian brothers and sisters throughout the ages, forgiveness for having carelessly torn your tunic, for having cut it up into so many pieces, or for having kept it this way because of indifference.

At the same time, we cannot help but nurture a fervent hope in your mercy, which is always greater than any of our sins and capable not only of forgiving, but also of forgetting.

Just as we cannot deny that we have a great faith in your immense love, which is able to draw good from every evil, if we believe in you and if we love you.

All this burns in our hearts, Jesus, in this moment, together with gratitude for what Christians of many Churches have been able to do, with your grace, for almost a century. Prompted by the Holy Spirit, they have worked toward mutual reconciliation through a fruitful dialogue of love, intense theological work, and a general raising of people's awareness of the need for unity.

And so, allow us to tell you, Lord, that although still in the acutely painful situation of not yet having achieved full communion, we sense in our heart the Christian optimism that your infinite Love cannot help but kindle.

We begin our work then, confident that you, who know how to conquer the world, will help us to help you fulfill your testament here on earth one day. Then, with unity achieved, your testament will witness to the world that you are the King and Lord of all hearts and peoples. Amen.

4
Unity and Jesus Crucified and Forsaken: Foundation of a Spirituality of Communion

Address to the World Council of Churches in Geneva on 28 October 2002.

Unity and Jesus forsaken, as you may know, constitute the two main principles and the foundation of the "spirituality of unity" that animates the Focolare Movement, this modern gift of the Spirit that was born in the Catholic Church, but that now includes Christians of more than 350 Churches and ecclesial communities.

The spirituality of unity is considered, also beyond the Movement itself, as an ecumenical spirituality.

The spirituality of unity is known today, especially in the Catholic Church, by the name "spirituality of communion," ever since John Paul II proposed it to the entire Catholic Church on 6 January 2001 in his Apostolic Letter *Novo Millennio Ineunte*. He invited everyone, on all levels, to live it.

Unity and Jesus forsaken are two great mysteries that are very closely connected!

Let's begin with unity.

What is unity?

The World Council of Churches has reflected on this subject since its birth.

Today unity is seen as a sign of the times, that is, a present-day need for both civic and religious society.

For those who have the Christian faith, unity is nothing less than God's plan for humanity, one united family of brothers and sisters, children of the same Father.

People without any religious affiliation also see the need for unity, because they are convinced that, in spite of the tensions and wars still raging, the world is moving toward unity.

This drive toward unity can be seen in the religious field, and as one instance there is the phenomenon of ecumenism after centuries of indifference if not conflict among the Churches. Similarly it can be seen in the political and social arenas, such as the unity between various European states or, with different aims, the unity sought in South America and in Africa.

As one aspect of this present-day worldwide movement toward unity there is the Focolare Movement with its special gift of the Spirit, its charism.

An important moment for the Movement was during World War II, in Trent (Italy), when some of my companions and I were in a cellar during an air-raid. We opened the Gospel at random and came upon Jesus' prayer for unity. It appeared to us in a new light: "Father, may they all be one" (see Jn 17:21). Those rather difficult words were lit up for us (an effect, we believe, of the charism we had received). We were able to understand them, while we felt certain in our hearts that that page was the *Magna Carta* of the emerging Movement.

Nevertheless, knowing that it would be difficult to put those words into practice, we asked Jesus, with faith, for the grace to learn how to live them.

And quite soon we realized — through a particular circumstance — that our prayer had been granted. The Holy Spirit revealed to us the true "secret," he showed us the precious "key" for accomplishing unity. It is Jesus crucified who cried out: "My God, my God, why have you forsaken me?" (Mt 27:46).

In fact, it became clear to us that Jesus had suffered that tremendous sense of abandonment, that sense of separation from the Father, precisely in order to re-unite all human beings to God, detached as they had been by sin, and to re-unite them to one another. It was evident, therefore, that that boundless suffering had something to do with the mystery of unity.

But he did not remain in the abyss of that infinite suffering. With unimaginable, immense effort he re-abandoned himself to the Father ("Father, into your hands I commend my spirit" — Lk 23:46). Thus he taught us how to face the most varied forms of disunity, separation, abandonment, that is, he taught us the way to overcome them.

Jesus forsaken, then, is another great mystery that I would like to consider now in depth (and also because I know that this is of interest to you).

First of all, we can ask ourselves: "What does Scripture say about Jesus forsaken? Who is he for theologians, for mystics of the past or of the present?"

The gospels are the first to speak of this suffering of Jesus, like that of Matthew: "From noon on, darkness came over the whole land until three in the afternoon. And about three o'clock Jesus cried with a loud voice, '*Eli, Eli, lema sabachthani?*' that is, 'My God, my God, why have you forsaken me?" ... The earth shook, and the rocks were split. The tombs also were opened' (Mt 27: 45–52). Also Paul mentions Jesus' abandonment when he affirms that "he made him to be sin" (see 2 Cor 5:21) although not a sinner.

This aspect of Jesus' passion was no longer mentioned after the apostolic age.

It was only centuries later that some mystics and theologians began to speak of him.

In the sixteenth century John of the Cross writes: "[At] the moment of his death, he was likewise annihilated in his soul, and was deprived of any relief and consolation, since his Father left him in the most intense aridity, according to the lower part of his nature. Wherefore he had perforce to cry out, saying: "My God! My God! Why hast thou forsaken me?" This was the greatest desolation, with respect to sense, that he had suffered in his life."[1]

Having generated us in that cry, it is here that the Church is born, the new people. Here the Holy Spirit is given. This is the Holy Spirit who, as God, binds Jesus to the Father. And in his forsakenness Jesus' link with the Father was obscured. As Louis Chardon affirms: "The Holy Spirit, being the true Paraclete, that is, the perfect consoler ... works in the soul [of Jesus] a more dreadful cross [than the exterior one],

---

1. St. John of the Cross, *The Ascent of Mount Carmel*, (London 1953) 3rd Revised Edition, trans. E. Allison Peers II, 7, 11.

with the suspension of all the marvelous consolations he had given."[2]

Among contemporary theologians, Sergei Bulgakov of the Orthodox Church affirms: "[In the forsakenness of Jesus] the inseparability itself of the most Holy Trinity appears broken, the Son is left alone.... This is the divine death, because "my soul is sorrowful even unto death," even unto the spiritual death which is abandonment by God."[3]

And the same theologian adds: "The cup is drained to the dregs, and the Son renders up his spirit to the Father: the most Holy Trinity restores itself to indivisible unity."[4]

And Karl Barth says: "God does not hold on to the booty, like a robber who keeps hold of the bag, he gives himself. Such is the glory of his Godhead, that he can be 'selfless'."[5]

The Ecumenical Patriarch of Constantinople, Bartholomew I, says: "Jesus, the Incarnate Word, covered the greatest distance that lost humanity could cover. 'My God, my God, why have you forsaken me?' An infinite distancing, the supreme torment, a prodigy of love. Between God and God, between the Father and the incarnate Word, is placed our despair with which Jesus is in solidarity right to its deepest depths."[6]

2. L. Chardon, O.P., *La croix de Jésus*, (Paris 1895) pp.262, 264.

3. S. Bulgakov, *L'Agnello di Dio*, (Rome, 1990), p.433.

4. *Ibid.*

5. K. Barth, *Dogmatics in Outline*, (London 1949) trans. G. T. Thomson, p. 166).

6. Ecumenical Patriarch Bartholomew of Constantinople, *Comment to the "Via Crucis"* at the Coliseum, 1 April 1994, in Osservatore Romano, 3 April 1994, p. 7

The Apostolic Letter of John Paul II, *Novo Millennio Ineunte,* speaks of Jesus' abandonment as *"the most paradoxical aspect of this mystery."* We read: "Is it possible to imagine a greater agony, a more impenetrable darkness?" And immediately afterwards: "In reality, the anguished 'why' addressed to the Father in the opening words of the Twenty-second Psalm expresses all the realism of unspeakable pain; but it is also illuminated by the meaning of that entire prayer, in which the Psalmist brings together suffering and trust."[7]

These, then, are some past and present thoughts on Jesus forsaken.

He presented himself to us not only in order to be contemplated, but above all as the model to imitate in all trials, and especially — we must say so at once — in the sufferings of disunity.

With regard to trials in general, the theologian Karl Rahner specifies: "To me it seems the Crucified One must have had all trials passing before his eyes at the time when he called out on the cross, without pietistic ideologies, 'My God, my God, why have you forsaken me?' ... tacitly meaning, though with a generous soul: 'Father, into your hands I commend my spirit'. " (Lk 23:46)[8]

In fact every kind of physical, moral or spiritual pain is nothing but a shadow of his immense pain.

Jesus Forsaken is the figure of everyone who is perplexed, full of doubt, of all those who ask "why."

---

7. *Novo millennio ineunte,* 25.

8. K. Rahner, *La grazia come libertà,* Alba, 1970, p.267.

Jesus forsaken is the image of the dumb. He can no longer speak; he does not know what to say except "*et nescivi*": "and I did not understand" (Ps 73:22).

Urs von Balthasar explains: "The interrogative is the only mode left for speech.... That loud cry is the word which is no longer a word, which cannot even be understood and explained as a word. It is less than a word ..., that which is chosen by the power of heaven ... to become the bearer of the eternal more-than-a-word."[9]

In a certain sense, Jesus forsaken is the figure of the blind — he does not see; of the deaf — he does not hear.

He is the exhausted one who complains.

He seems given over to despair.

He is one who starves ... for union with God.

He is the image of the deceived, the fearful, the bewildered. He appears to have failed.

Jesus forsaken is the image of darkness, melancholy, conflict; the image of all that is indefinable, strange, because he is a God who cries for help! He is non-sense.

Again Urs von Balthasar says: "The Son, completely forsaken by people as also by God, hangs between heaven and earth, and he takes upon himself the darkness of the world's guilt, which veils and blocks from view any possibility of meaning and of effect for his pain, since sin, in relation to God's love given in vain, is without meaning and without reason."[10]

---

9. H. U. von Balthasar, *Il tutto nel frammento* (Milan, 1990), pp.247–249.

10. H. U. von Balthasar, *Teodrammatica* IV:331.

Jesus forsaken is the one who is lonely, the derelict.... He appears useless, cast aside, in shock....

And in all of these sufferings, which we can experience personally, we can recognize him.

But we can see him also in every brother and sister who suffers.

We see him in the situations of poverty we encounter.

And what happens when we encounter these living images of Jesus forsaken?

In approaching those who resemble him, we can openly speak to them of him. For all who recognize their similarity to him and accept a share in his fate, this is how he turns out to be: speech for the mute, the answer for the ignorant, light for the blind, a voice for the deaf, rest for the weary, hope for the despairing, satisfaction for the hungry, reality for the deceived, victory for the failure, courage for the fearful, joy for the sorrowful, certainty for the uncertain, normality for the strange, company for the lonely, unity for the separated, that which is uniquely useful for the useless.

The rejected feel chosen. Jesus forsaken is peace for the restless, a home for the evicted, reunion for the outcast.

Because of him, people are reborn, and the senselessness of suffering acquires meaning.

As the Church Fathers say: "All that was assumed was redeemed." And the theologian Karl Rahner comments: "For it became the life and destiny of God himself. He assumed death; therefore death must be something more than a sunset into a meaningless void. He assumed the state of being forsaken; therefore loneliness contains in itself the promise of a happy and divine closeness. He assumed lack of success; therefore defeat can be a victory. He assumed abandonment by God; therefore God is close even when we think we have been forsaken by him. He assumed all; therefore all is redeemed."[11]

Jesus forsaken should be loved especially when dealing with those who appear to be sinners or enemies.

We also recognize any painful event as one of his faces.

For instance, whenever someone who seemed to be indispensable is no longer present, we feel a little like him without his Father's support; he who had said, "I am not alone because the Father is with me" (Jn 16:32).

In moments like these, Jesus forsaken is our only support.

We can also experience divisions, both large and small, in the communities we live in, in our families, groups, offices, centers, schools, etc., and this makes us suffer. There too, we can see him and personally overcome that suffering within ourselves and do all we can to recompose unity with the others.

The same applies to larger communities like those of our Churches. Imitating him, we can recompose unity in them, between various persons, among different groups, and so on.

11. K. Rahner, Misteri della vita di Cristo, Ecce homo!; in Nuovi Saggi II (Rome, 1968) II:173–174.

Jesus forsaken is also the light for recomposing the full visible communion of the one Church of Christ. We can see him as the "ecumenical crucified one."

What is the best way to overcome every disunity, whether personal or collective?

In both cases, I must say this: "If he has taken upon himself every suffering, every division and trauma, I can think that wherever I see a suffering, I also see him. This suffering reminds me of him; it's a presence of his, a face of his."

And like him, we too must not stop in the cracks of division. If Jesus re-abandoned himself to the Father who was abandoning him, in like manner we must go beyond and overcome the trial, saying: "In this suffering, I love you, Jesus forsaken, I want you, I embrace you!"

And if we are so willing, generous and attentive to continue loving what God wants from us in the following moment, we experience that, more often than not, the suffering disappears, as if by a divine alchemy. It's because love calls forth the gifts of the Spirit: joy, light, peace, and the risen Lord in us takes the place of the forsaken one.

And what fruits come from loving Jesus forsaken whom we recognize in the lack of full communion among our Churches?

There are very many. First of all, the unity among Churches that it has been possible to achieve so far, is a strong witness to the Gospel, in which the painful fact of the not perfect and visible communion and its consequences are faced with constructive courage and peace.

At this point, however, I hope you will be happy, Ladies and Gentlemen, to listen to a brief summary of our ecumenical history, because it was precisely out of love for Jesus forsaken that we launched ourselves into this adventure. The absurd divisions among Christians reminded us of his "why."

The first contacts of the Focolare Movement with the world of Christians of other Churches took place in Germany in 1961, when three Lutheran pastors, present at one of our meetings, were impressed by the fact that Catholics were speaking of the Gospel and above all, living it so intensely. They immediately invited us to bring our experience into their parishes and communities. An "exchange of gifts" began. We went to Germany, then they came to Rome, and together by loving Jesus crucified and forsaken present in the anomaly of our not being in full and visible communion, a sincere, candid and genuine fraternity was born among us.

We decided to begin a Centre of shared life between Catholics and Lutherans in Ottmaring, near Augsburg in Germany, with the permission of the respective bishops: Hermann Dietzfelbinger, Evangelical, and Joseph Stimpfle, Catholic, a center which is today — after 30 years of life — a recognized and valued ecumenical meeting place, an ecumenical "little town."

Later on, some Anglican priests who had participated in one of our meetings for Catholics and Evangelical Lutherans were touched by the warm and serene atmosphere they found among everyone.

They organized an audience for me in London with the Primate of the Church of England, Michael Ramsey, who said to me: "I see the hand of God in this Work," and he invited me to establish the Movement in his Church, greatly in need of unity. His successors, Archbishops Coggan, Runcie and Carey were of the same opinion.

In June, 1967, the Ecumenical Patriarch Athenagoras I in Istanbul wished to learn more about our Movement. He was struck by the love that is lived, by Christianity become life, but also by the importance given to Mary, the most perfect follower of Christ.

Through him, the spirit of the Focolare Movement spread among the Orthodox of the Middle East, and then everywhere.

Patriarch Dimitrios I, who succeeded Athenagoras I, and the present Patriarch, His Holiness Bartholomew I, continue to have a relationship of mutual esteem and cooperation with us.

Later on, this spirituality of unity was welcomed by the Syrian Orthodox, the Armenian Orthodox, the Coptic Orthodox, the Ethiopian Orthodox and the Assyrian Church of the East.

Also members of the Reformed Church here in Switzerland and in Holland came into contact with us, as well as Baptists, Methodists, Mennonites and many others, struck by different aspects of our spirituality.

Now, after forty years of ecumenical life in the Movement, we can see the lines of a specific contribution in the ecumenical field based precisely on the spirituality of unity.

With brothers and sisters of the various Churches, striving to live the Gospel together, getting to know one another, reinforcing our reciprocal love, we have discovered the great wealth of our common heritage: Baptism, the Old and New Testaments, the dogmas of the first Councils which we share, the Creed (Nicene-Constantinopolitan), the Greek and Latin Fathers, the martyrs and other things, like the life of grace, faith, hope, charity, and the many other inner gifts of the Holy Spirit. And besides all this, we are united by the spirituality of unity.

At first we lived as if all this were not really true or we were not fully aware of it. But now we realize that they are the conditions for being able to achieve a particular dialogue: the dialogue of life.

Because of it we feel that we are already one family; we feel that we form among ourselves "a Christian people" which includes lay people, but also priests, pastors, bishops, and so on.

Obviously, the full and visible communion among our Churches still needs to be achieved, but we can already live this reality.

It is not a base or grassroots dialogue that runs contrary to or merely alongside that of official representatives or the Church leaders, but a dialogue in which all Christians can participate.

This people is like leaven in the ecumenical Movement that awakens in everyone the sense that, as baptized Christians capable of loving one another, we can all contribute toward realizing the Testament of Jesus.

Indeed, we hope that other forms of dialogue, like that of charity, of shared service, of prayer, the theological dialogue, can be empowered by the "dialogue of life."

We also hope that the perennial problem of how people receive the progress made in the official theological dialogues, may be overcome by a people who are ecumenically educated.

This spirituality also offers the possibility of opening dialogues with those who do not know Christ.

John Paul II wrote to the Bishops, friends of the Focolare Movement, in February 2001: "Love for the crucified Christ, viewed in the culminating moment of his suffering and forsakenness, constitutes the best way... also to initiate a fruitful dialogue with other cultures and religions."

Upheld as always by love for Jesus forsaken, in 1977 we began our interreligious dialogue.

The event which, in a certain sense, marked the beginning of this dialogue, took place in London, in the Guildhall, during a speech I gave to an audience of representatives from the major world religions.

As I was leaving the hall, the first people who came to greet me were Jews, Buddhists, Sikhs, Hindus, Muslims....

This happens because the Movement has spread all over the world, and so people come to know something about us. The focolarini are in contact with many faithful of other religions, whom they love, and they in turn feel attracted and want to know more about us.

Two years later we had a meeting with a distinguished Buddhist leader, Rev. Nikkyo Niwano, founder in Japan of a flourishing lay association of six million members, the Rissho Kosei-kai. He invited me to Tokyo to speak about my Christian experience to ten thousand Buddhists in their Great Sacred Hall.

But the most surprising contacts with Buddhism came a few years ago in Italy and in Thailand with eminent representatives of Theravada monasticism and with hundreds of their disciples.

This is what happened: a Buddhist Great Teacher and one of his disciples, a learned and open person, had met members of the Movement in Asia and wanted to know more about us. They decided to visit Loppiano, one of our little towns near Florence. They were deeply moved by the evangelical love they found there.

Afterwards, the disciple came to see me in Rome and he confessed: "I've studied very, very much. I loved Buddha because he was beautiful, luminous, like a sun, surrounded by lotuses, whereas I didn't even want to look at Jesus, who was ugly, covered with blood and dirty. Now I've understood: he is the 'super-love'."

Later on he and the Great Teacher, enthusiastic about the experience they had lived, invited me to speak to their followers.

So I went to Thailand to share my experience in Chiang Mai (in the north of the country) to students and teachers of a Buddhist University, and in a temple, to Buddhist monks, nuns and lay people.

Now this dialogue is spreading in an incredible way, in many parts of the country, and the fraternity between us is something very real.

What lays the foundations for fraternity among people of different religions is the discovery of the so-called "Golden Rule," present in the Sacred Books of the main religions. It says: "Do to others what you would have them do to you" (Lk 6:31), which means: love. By living this, we obey the Gospel and so we love them, and they love us. The result is brotherhood.

With regard to the dialogue with Islam too, our first contact was casual.

Today some seven thousand Muslim friends are in contact with the Movement in Asia, in Africa, in America and also in Europe. In our spirituality they find things that give incentive and affirmation that helps them live out and adhere more deeply to the heart of their Islamic spirituality, and for some, to their mysticism.

A few years ago we met an Imam, W. D. Mohammed, who is head of a peaceful Movement of two million African Americans.

I, a white Christian woman, was called to speak to three thousand of his African American Muslims in the Malcolm Shabazz Mosque of Harlem, New York. They gave me their utmost attention.

Then we had a number of important meetings with them in Rome and one big event in Washington, D.C.

Now, since we are spread in many parts of the United States, they have invited us to speak in forty of their mosques, so that we can present our Christian experiences in which they are very interested.

Speaking of the Abrahamic religions, I must also mention the various contacts we have had with Jewish brothers and sisters in several parts of the world, as in Buenos Aires, where we met with one of their numerous communities.

In the past two years a promising dialogue with some Hindus in India has begun. We have friendly and profound contacts with Gandhian Movements in Coimbatore and others which are very numerous and important, especially in Mumbai.

This year we had a Hindu-Christian Symposium in Rome during which we were able to communicate many Christian truths.

Now there are tens of thousands of members of other religions who share, as far as possible, the spirituality and aims of the Movement.

We are giving our contribution so that the religious pluralism of humanity may lose more and more of the negative elements which can foment divisions and wars, and acquire, in the conscience of millions of women and men, the awareness of a challenge: that of working to build together universal fraternity.

This does not exclude the fact that there are still crucial questions to be resolved, which form an essential part of Christian thought, factors that stimulate theological exchange and deepen it.

But there is great hope, especially due to the presence in all of these religions of the so-called "seeds of the Word" ("seeds of the Word which lie hidden among them")[12]. In the future, these truths which we highlight will open to many the knowledge of Christ.

Finally, we also have a profound experience with people of other cultural backgrounds that are not based on religion, in whom we see, more clearly than ever, the face of Jesus forsaken who is "searching," or who is "reduced to being a mere man" or the figure of the "non-believer," of the "atheist," etc.

These people do not reject the idea of kindness and good will toward all, because love of neighbor is written in the DNA of every man and woman, and, like everyone else, they are attracted by the idea of working toward a universal family, a more united world. With them, we also seek to highlight shared values like justice, peace, freedom, human rights, solidarity, and so forth, and to work together so that such values may prevail.

In the dialogues I have just mentioned we rely first of all on witness and then on the spoken word.

And our witness ranges from living mutual love (so that the words regarding the early Christians can be applied to us too: "See how they love one another and how they are ready to die for one another,"[13]) to loving everyone also by promoting social works and activities aimed at resolving the specific sufferings that devastate various countries, as practical expressions of our love.

---

12. Ad gentes, 11.

13. Tertullian, Apologetico, testo latino, traduzione e note di Anna Resta Barrile, Bologna,1980, cap. 39,7, p.145.

Our dialogue is carried out in this way: first of all, we put ourselves on the same level as our partner, whoever he or she may be: then we listen, emptying ourselves completely, as Jesus forsaken teaches, in *kenosis*. This enables us to receive the other person within ourselves and to understand him or her, while we also receive a very useful inculturation.

After having been listened to with love, the other person is willing to listen in turn to what we have to say, our so-called "respectful announcement" of the truths we believe in. At this point the dialogue flows into evangelization without ever forcing anything on anyone, but only to be faithful to God and consistent with ourselves.

In conclusion, we can bear witness to the fact that love for Jesus forsaken has won every battle in and outside of ourselves, even the most terrible. But certainly, we have had to be totally his, we have had to give ourselves to him completely.

And it was only love for him that enabled us to build a Movement so rich, so variegated, so vast, aimed at the one goal that by now we all are aware of: unity, with all the meanings this divine word implies, open to an all-encompassing fraternity.

5
Living the Word — Way to Unity

Address given during the 21st ecumenical meeting of bishops friends of the Focolare Movement, held at Morges in Switzerland

The topic I will develop today, "the Word of God," is inexhaustibly rich and fundamentally important for all Christians, and I would say that it is especially so for us, members of the Focolare Movement, called by God to radiate — along with other modern ecclesial realities — a radical and genuine life of the Gospel.

And I am very happy to speak about God's Word here in Geneva because I know that for the Churches of the Reformation, the Word is a stronghold, the pillar on which they are founded.

In speaking about the Word, I will refer to my experience and to that of the Movement I represent, described some time ago by the Anglican Archdeacon Bernard Pawley, observer to the Second Vatican Council, as "a spring of living water surging forth from the Gospel."

So I will share with you briefly how the Lord led us to giving the utmost importance to the Gospel and to living it, thus finding infinite treasures in it.

But first of all, what is the Word of God?

I remember that one day the answer became very clear to me when I read this passage in the Gospel: "They were yours, and you gave them to me, and they have kept your word. Now they know that everything you have given me is from you; for the words that you gave to me I have given to them, and they have received them and know in truth that I came from you; and they have believed that you sent me" (Jn 17:6–8). In reading these words I clearly understood in the depths of my soul that the phrases "your word," "everything you gave me," "the words you gave to me," and "I came from you" were somehow synonymous, that is, that the words pronounced by Jesus were Jesus himself, the Word pronounced from all eternity by the Father.

It was a discovery of heady excitement, and I wanted to find it confirmed in Augustine of Hippo's commentary on the passage.

Here it is: "Everything the Father has given to the Son, he has given it in generating him.... In what other way would he give some words to the Word, since in the Word he has said everything in an ineffable way?"[1]

I was therefore in agreement with Augustine.

But let us proceed in an orderly fashion, and start out from the early years of the Focolare Movement's history and from the first experiences that the Lord had us live with regard to the Word of God.

I was young and I was hungry for truth. My ideal was studying, especially philosophy. Searching for

---

1. *Commento al Vangelo di S. Giovanni*, Disc. CVI, 7, Rome 1974, vol. II, p.417.

the truth with ancient and modern philosophers was
what fully satisfied my mind and my heart. Then one
day, a new understanding came to me. "How can it
be," I asked myself, "that you are searching for the
truth? Isn't there someone who said that he himself
is the truth in person? Didn't Jesus say of himself: 'I
am the truth?' (see Jn 14:6)."

This, then, was one of the first reasons that
prompted me to search for the truth not so much in
books, but in Jesus.

And I decided to follow him.

The terrible difficulties we were exposed to every
day in 1943, in Trent, my native city, due to the Second World War, were the circumstances that at that
time led the first members of our newly-born Movement to take a new approach to the Gospel. We read
it whenever we could.

And because of a grace that was undoubtedly
special, linked to the charism God had given us, the
words of God appeared to be remarkably new, as if
we had never known them before. Unlike all that is
written by human beings, these words proved to be
unique, unfathomable resources. They were eternal
words, which meant that they were relevant for all
times, and therefore, also for our times. They were
universal words for people of every race and nation.
Jesus revealed himself to us as the true light that en-
lightens everyone (see Jn 1:9).

Jesus in fact had risen: he was alive and present; this was our conviction, as it was in the early
Church. And if Jesus had risen and was alive, his
words — even though spoken in the past — were

not simply records of the past, but words he was addressing today to all of us and to each person of every age.

"Love your neighbor as yourself" (Mt 19:19). Yes, everyone could live those words, but who among us actually lived in this way? Who loved their neighbor *as* themselves?

"Love your enemies, do good to those who hate you" (Lk 6:27). Who did this?

We called ourselves Christians, but our enemy, however large or small, often remained so for the rest of our lives.

Moreover, the words of the Gospel were words of life that could immediately be put into practice. We began to live them and a revolution was born: the revolution of the Gospel.

All our relationships changed: with our neighbors and with God. People who had ignored one another before became a family; Christians who were indifferent to one another before, came together as one.

Taking the Word seriously and living it radically, gave rise to a community: it was the newly-born Focolare Movement.

People from the outside observing this phenomenon were surprised to find — rather than merely a Word of the Gospel being read and meditated on — a living Christian community. And they sometimes wondered what strange meditations on God's Word we had been doing.

And because we sought to fulfill his words to the letter, he responded by fulfilling the Gospel promises to the letter. "If you abide in me, and my words abide in you," Jesus had said, "ask for whatever you wish, and it will be done for you" (Jn 15:7). What we asked for, we were given.

God looked after us even more than the birds of the air and the lilies of the field. For the little we gave to him, he gave back to us in great abundance. For the little we left because of him, we received a hundred times as much.

The Gospel thus became "the" book. We wrote at that time: "We have no other book but the Gospel; we have no other science, no other art. There, is Life! Whoever finds it does not die."[2]

Quite soon you could find people with the Gospel in their hands in almost all the air-raid shelters along the hillsides surrounding the city of Trent.

How watered down other books appeared to us at that time, even the beautiful spiritual books we had previously read and meditated on! How many pages one often had to read before finding an idea that could be put into practice! And how the theories of philosophers seemed to fade away, theories that previously had had a degree of fascination for us students!

Instead, every word of Jesus was like a beam of brilliant light: totally divine!

We took one complete sentence of the Gospel; we meditated on it; we wrote a commentary that we wished to have confirmed by those who represented the Church for us, and we lived it. By doing so, the Lord — as we understood much later — was putting into our hands "the alphabet to know Christ" (as we

---

2. Letter from 1948.

called it). We need just a few letters and just a few
grammar rules — we would say — in order to know
how to read and write. But if we do not know them
we remain illiterate for the rest of our lives.

And just as the body breathes in order to live,
so the soul in order to remain alive must live the
Word of God. Living it: this is what the Holy Spirit
was mainly urging us to do. It was an inner voice
that was re-echoing what had already been written:
"Be doers of the word, and not merely hearers who
deceive themselves" (Jas 1:22). Or "Everyone then
who hears these words of mine and acts on them
will be like a wise man who built his house on rock"
(Mt 7:24). The conviction God had given us in this
regard was so strong and we felt such an urgent need
to act upon it, that we repeated this thought: "If, as
an absurd hypothesis, all the Gospels on earth were
destroyed, we would like to live in such a way that
people, seeing our actions, could, in a sense, re-write
the Gospel: "Blessed are you who weep now, for you
will laugh" (Lk 6:21), "Blessed are the merciful, for
they will receive mercy" (Mt 5:7). "Do not judge"
(Mt 7:1); "Love your enemies" (Mt 5:44).

But we were not living the Word of God only
individually, each one on his or her own. The useful
experiences, the insights, and the graces received by
living the Word were put in common. They had to
be put in common because of the mutual love that is
the fundamental law of our Movement. As a result,
those who listened to an experience derived benefit
from it and those who spoke were enriched by it.

We felt it was our duty to share with others what we were undergoing, also because we realized that whenever we gave others our experience it remained and served to build up our own inner life, while if we failed to give it our souls were gradually impoverished.

So, the Word of God was lived intensely throughout the day. And then the fruits would be communicated among us and also with the people who joined the initial group.

The Word was like a password that everyone wanted to hold on to in order to be sure of being included in the newly-born community.

What was emerging from this was really something new. To understand this well we must bear in mind that before this happy moment, a moment of special enlightenment by the Holy Spirit about the Word of God, we were not used to living the Word of God like this, that is, applying it to all the circumstances of our lives and sharing the effects with one another. We used to meditate on the Word of God, penetrate it with our mind, see if we could derive some thoughts from it, and, if we were fervent, make some resolutions.

This was something completely different. Now the Word of God was being examined to discern the various ways of putting it into practice in the course of daily life and it began to transform each individual and the group as a whole. When we were living it, it was no longer "I" or "we" who lived, but the Word in me, the Word in the group of us.

And today, almost sixty years later, it is still like this. We feel that it is absolutely necessary that the Word of God become our way of life.

Now there are people in the Movement who dedicate themselves to biblical studies and exegesis with commitment and competence. But the Spirit urges us always and above all to live the Word. And communicating our experiences on the Word still brings an advantage we cannot overlook if we consider the environment in which we are called to live out our Christian life. In the midst of the noise and turmoil of the modern world, accentuated by the media which pollutes the atmosphere with subjects that are purely mundane, if not downright harmful, people learn to fill their hours with heavenly conversations and in this way do what Paul asked: "Seek the things that are above.... Set your minds on things that are above, not on things that are on earth" (Col 3:1–2).

Those who belong to the Movement, furthermore, do not consider living the Word of God to be only a practice that, individually and as a community, maintains their spiritual tone. It is also a "fount of God" from which they can drink. With it and through it, they feel that they can be nourished with God as when they draw from the other divine sources that their Church offers, like the Eucharist, for example. As the Second Vatican Council would emphasize strongly twenty years later, the members of the Movement had always been aware of the need to be nourished on God with the Eucharist, but also with the Word, just as it had been during the early times of the Church. "We eat his flesh and drink his blood in the divine Eucharist, but also in the reading of the Scriptures," said St. Jerome.[3]

---

3. St. Jerome, *Commentarius in Ecclesiastern,* III, 13; Corpus Christianorum Series Latina LXXII (Turnholdt, 1959), p.278.

In addition, we consider the Word of God like clothes we put on every day so that we can always be living examples of the doctrine of Christ. "Put on the Lord Jesus Christ" (Rom 13:14), says Paul. Dressed like this, the members of the Movement show the world what it means to be sons and daughters of God according to the Gospel. It is clothing that protects and keeps alight the fire of grace and charity. The Word preserves them from all that, within or without, which is an obstacle to union with God. Above all, it puts them on the offensive, and not just on the defensive, in relation to the world.

If we observe the members of the Movement who live the Word of God, we notice a wide variety of effects which the Word produces in them. In fact, the situations people find themselves in are infinitely various, and infinitely various are the applications of the Word in the life of each person, and infinitely various, therefore, are the results. If we had to list the effects the Word produces, we would never finish. We will point out only a few, in addition to those already mentioned.

First of all, the Word of God brings about a change of mentality. It instills in the hearts of everyone (Europeans, Asians, Australians, Americans, Africans), the sentiments of Christ in dealing with circumstances, individuals and society.

Whoever is in contact with an environment where the Word is lived as it should be by individuals and by the community, can discover another effect: they realize that in that environment one lives on a supernatural level. In fact, the Word of God makes us fully alive. As Paul says: Life [is brought] ... to light through the gospel (see 2 Tm 1:10).

The Word of God also sets us free: "The truth will make you free" (Jn 8:32) affirms the Gospel. The truth sets us free because in those who live it, Christ lives, the "new self"; and consequently, the "old self" is dead: we are no longer slaves to our old nature (see Eph 4:22–24; Col 3:9). We are free from ourselves.

But the Word frees us also because we are no longer slaves of human conditioning. We love Christ in everyone and, by the grace of God, we do not expect anything from anyone.

In addition, the Word frees us from being oppressed by circumstances. In fact, nothing happens by chance or merely because it is willed by human beings. The Father is always present in our lives, either because he wills something to happen, or because he permits it to happen.

Still other effects: the Word gives joy, it gives happiness, it gives peace, it gives fullness, it gives light. The Spirit bestows his gifts in people's hearts because the new self lives. And the joy, peace and light, so characteristic of our Movement and fruits of the Word, are forces that extend the kingdom of God. As a matter of fact, on seeing groups of the Movement, people wonder and want to know the cause of these effects. And once they have discovered it, more often than not, they wish to live it out as well.

Another effect is that the Word purifies. A type of rejuvenation takes place in the persons who live the Word.

Other effects: the Word leads to conversions to God and vocations of the most varied types to follow him. Through the Word, some feel called to virginity, some to the priesthood, some to the religious life or to a service in their Church, and some to marriage that is a "little domestic Church."

The Word also produces concrete works. For many years we have been spectators of this rather than actors, beholding the various works produced by the members of our Movement. "Like a tree planted by a stream of water," John Damascene would say, "so also the soul, watered by the divine Scriptures, grows and prospers ... and is always adorned with green leaves, that is, works which are beautiful in the eyes of God."[4]

Another fruit of the Word is that it brings about union with God. When people develop the habit of living the Word of God, within themselves they become aware of communion with Jesus. They speak to him with ease; they call upon him in times of need; they rejoice in his presence in the depths of their soul. In short, through the Word, the small tree of the inner life begins to grow in their hearts.

Yet another fruit of the Word is that it gives us hope of eternal life. Because we see all the promises of the Gospel come true every day, one by one, we feel certain that one day, through the Word, the gate of heaven will open. As Jesus said: "the hundredfold in this life and eternal life" (Lk 18:29).

Another fruit of the Word is that it makes us one: it brings about unity. Just as when the two living parts

---

4. St. John Damascene, *De Fide Ortodoxa*, lib.IV, c.17; PG94:1175B.

of branches that are stripped of their bark come into contact and become one, likewise, when two souls "stripped" of all that is merely human by living the Word of Life, come into contact, they too are better consumed into one.

Those who do not live the Word of God bring a merely human atmosphere wherever they go. They will not bring society together, but they will become a cause of discord and division. This is what Cyprian feared. In his treatise *De unitate*, he dealt principally with the unity of the Church, but he did not fail to urge us over and over again to live the Gospel. He said that it was precisely because the Gospel was not lived that there were schisms in the Church.

But all the effects we have listed here have their origin in one essential fact. As we know, the Word of God is not like other words. Not only does the Word tell us something, but it also has the power to bring about what it says. The Word, which is a presence of Christ, generates Christ in our souls and in the souls of others.

It is true that even before living the Word with commitment, we are Christians, we possess the life of Christ, and with it we undoubtedly have the light and love of God. But we are a bit like a caterpillar, still closed up in a cocoon. When we live the Gospel, love radiates light in us and this light makes our love grow. It is like the caterpillar in the cocoon that has started moving and changing until it comes out as a butterfly. We can say that Christ starts to live in us, and then he grows more and more in us so that we become evermore filled with him.

Paul VI has given a magnificent description of what the Word produces. He says: "How does Jesus become present in our souls? The divine thought, the Word, the Son of God made man, comes through this vehicle: the communication of the Word. We could assert that the Lord incarnates himself within us when we allow his Word to come and live within us."[5]

We could go on and on. In brief, the life of the Word brings about a complete re-evangelization of people's way of thinking, of willing, of loving. The Gospel, the law of life, is incarnated. It is not a book like other books. Wherever it takes root, as we said before, it gives rise to the Christian revolution because the Gospel gives laws, not only for the union of the soul with God, but also for the union of persons with one another, be they friends or enemies. The Gospel lays down as its supreme demand the unity of all, the last will of Jesus fulfilled, at least in that part of society where Christians live the Word.

The Testament of Jesus, his prayer for unity, chapter seventeen of John's Gospel: I remember this was one of the first pages of the Gospel we read. It was an event of huge importance for us. We still have vivid memories of how, as we moved from one word to the next, each one seemed to light up. And

---

5. From the discourse of Paul VI to the parish of St. Eusebius, 26 February 1967.

now we understand that it was as if someone were saying to us: "Look, you must learn many things in school, but the summary of it all is this: 'sanctify them in the truth … may they all be one … you will have the fullness of joy… and you will be one as I am one with the Father'…" (see Jn 17:1–26). The Testament of Jesus seemed to us to be the summary of the Gospel. And we understood it with an awareness that could only be attributed to a special grace. Once we penetrated it — as and inasmuch as God willed — it became easier for us to understand the rest of the Gospel.

After five or six years of living many different words of the Gospel, it became clear to us that they were all similar. There was something that they all had in common. One had as much value as the other, because the effects of one in the soul were identical to those of the others.

The fact is that every Word, although expressed in human terms and in different ways, is the Word of God. But since God is Love, every Word is charity. We believe that we discovered during that period that beneath every Word was charity. And when one of these Words dropped into our soul, it seemed to be transformed into fire, into flames, to be transformed into love. We could affirm that our inner life was all love, and so everything was simplified.

It was contemplating the mystery of Jesus that most interested us, his being forsaken by the Father, that gave us the possibility of understanding that each Word of the Gospel contains the whole Gospel. As early as 1944 our attention had been drawn by

Jesus' cry on the cross, "My God, my God, why have you forsaken me" (Mt 27:46; Mk 15:34), and we had recognized in him the secret, the key for recomposing the unity that had been shattered by sin. As we grew in our love for him, we seemed to understand that there is a special relationship between the Gospel and Jesus crucified and forsaken. In fact, we saw in him the entire Gospel opened up, the Gospel completely disclosed, the Word par excellence. We understood that in that terrible trial, he had lived the Gospel in its entirety and in the greatest depth.

Looking specifically at each of Jesus' exhortations, we saw that he lived all of them in that moment.

Jesus forsaken relives in himself, at that instant, the words: "Whoever comes to me and does not put aside father and mother ... and even life itself" (see Lk 14:26).

Jesus forsaken can apply all the beatitudes to himself: he is poor, he is persecuted, he is meek, he is a peacemaker (he unites the disunited, and so on). The virtues are uniquely resplendent in Jesus forsaken: fortitude, patience, temperance, perseverance, justice, magnanimity…. In his forsakenness Jesus seems to be nothing but a man, and so never had he been as close to us human beings as in that moment and never, therefore, had he loved so much. At the same time, never had he been so close to the Father; it is out of love for him that he dies, and that he dies in that way. If "the Law and the Prophets" (Mt 7:12) consist in love of God and love of neighbor, Jesus here fulfilled completely every desire and commandment of God. Jesus forsaken is therefore the direct path to holiness, because he brings about unity with the Holy

One. Whoever focuses their heart completely on him finds ... the pure Gospel.

Then, by living the Word according to our spirituality, we had a new understanding of Mary. She, who "treasured all these things in her heart" (Lk 2:51), revealed herself to us as completely Word of God, all clothed with the Word of God. And if the Word is the beauty of the Father, Mary, given substance by the Word of God, was of incomparable beauty. And Mary's originality was, to perfection in her case, what should be true of every Christian: to repeat Christ, the Truth, the Word, with the personality that God has given him or her.

Each one of us (the idea of each one of us) is eternally in the Mind of God, in the Word.... Up there, each one is that Word of God which God has spoken from all eternity. And from all eternity his or her being is in the Being, and the idea of each of us (a Word of God) is in the Word, our life in the Life.

God has spoken each one of us from Himself, as eternally he has spoken His Son, because in seeing us in Himself he loved us and gave us life shaping us by the Holy Spirit.

I have recounted some of the effects that come to fruition by living the Word, a few discoveries that can be made, and several insights one can have.

But the Word is so powerful that it can lead us to other, undreamed-of effects, other discoveries, understandings, and other heights. Clement of Alexandria says: "Those who obey the Lord and follow the Scripture ... are fully transformed into the image of the Master: they come to live like God in the flesh. But this height cannot be reached by those who do not follow God's lead: and he leads through the divinely inspired Scriptures."[6]

I would like to share another experience. In the Movement we take one Word at a time and live it. We have experiences, often quite small ones, that tell us something the world doesn't tell us. In other words, we put into practice what Jesus asks us to do and the promises he makes us are verified.

St. Paul's publishing house in Italy asked us to gather together some of these experiences from all over the world. So we sent the first 60 that came to hand and the result was a book entitled *I fioretti*.[7]

I would like to recount three of them. One is called: *The Three Coats*. A mother with no money from New York had three small children and needed to buy three coats for them because their old ones were worn out. She did not have any money, but she saw in the newspaper that there was a shop offering coats at very low prices in a sale. So she said to herself: "I mustn't miss this opportunity; I have to go straightaway and buy three coats for the children." Just at that moment her mother-in-law rang. At first she thought: "I'll have to tell her I'm rushing out." But then she had another thought: "Jesus will take what I say to her as if I were saying it to him, because "whatever you do to the least ..." So, she forgot about the coats, with great sadness for her children, and said

---

6. Clement of Alexandria, Stromatum, VII, 16, PG9, 539 C.

7. Published in English by New City, as Glimpses of Gospel Life, London 2004.

to her mother-in-law: "Come round!" Eventually the mother-in-law arrived, rang the bell and the mother opened the door to her. The mother-in-law was carrying a large package. When she opened it up, guess what was inside! Three coats for the children.

Another story concerns a bishop in Argentina. "While I was on a daily walk as directed by my doctor, I was trying to get to know the area where I had been living for a short time. I was the new bishop. A few days later, I started to do some tidying up in the house. I found some bronze candelabras, which didn't really fit in. A small shop selling second hand goods, which I had seen on my walk, came to mind. I thought that, given the difficult economic conditions in the country, the owner might be in serious difficulties. I asked my secretary to parcel up the candelabras and give them to the shopkeeper with a card, which read: "These are a little gift from the bishop. If you manage to sell them, please give the money to the poor. But if you need them for yourself you can keep them." During the afternoon the man came to the bishop's house. He insisted on seeing me. When I met him he said to me, "Today I wanted to commit suicide, but when your secretary came, I realized that someone still cared for me, and I changed my mind. Many thanks!"

These are the kinds of things that happen. Here's another one. In the early times of the Movement it often happened that we would give an apple away, the only one we had in focolare, and we would then receive another twelve; we gave those way and perhaps a whole case would arrive. The Gospel was continuing … It was one of our great joys because such things seemed to us like Gospel facts.

And from New Zealand: "One Saturday morning someone came to pay us a short visit. When she was leaving, knowing that she had many children and that financially things weren't going too well, we gave her all our week's provisions. After a while another family visited us and, as they had been to the market, they offered us fresh apples and pears. We were happy because we saw it as the 'give, and it will be given to you' from the Gospel (Lk 6:38). In the afternoon, as an act of love, we had promised to go to a party organized by the local Italian Community. We had decided on the way to visit another needy family and take them all the apples and pears we had received. Once the party was over, before we left, the family who had invited us gave us a large box full of pears and apples from their orchard, all of excellent quality, along with a watermelon. We were delighted that these experiences should happen not only in the early days of the Movement, but today too."

Also available:

A Handbook of Spiritual Ecumenism
Cardinal Walter Kasper

This *Handbook* offers practical suggestions for implementing and strengthening spiritual ecumenism, the heart of all efforts to re-unite divided Christians. It is grounded in the documents that have shaped the Catholic Church's engagement in seeking Christian unity, those of the Second Vatican Council, as well as the encyclical *Ut Unum Sint* and the *Catechism of the Catholic Church*. It is written for anyone who values deeply the restoration of Christian unity, especially those responsible for promoting it at various levels of Church life.

ISBN 978-1-56548-263-0, paper, 96 pages

Also available:

Essential Writings
Spirituality · Dialogue · Culture
Chiara Lubich

"This selection and arrangement of Chiara Lubich's spiritual writings opens up the heart and soul of one of the most significant religious figures of our times. In our own day, there may be nothing more important than giving witness to the hope and the possibility of unity between and among people of all faiths — and of those with no faith at all. This is the legacy Chiara leaves to everyone concerned with the unity of all people."

Michael Downey, Editor
The New Dictionary of Catholic Spirituality

ISBN 978-1-56548-259-3, paper, 432 pages